Friend

Contents

School

You can make friends at school. Friends like each other. Friends help each other.

Friends talk to each other.
Friends play together in
the playground.

Home

Friends can come to visit you at home. Friends like doing things together.

Some things are easier to do with a friend. It's easier to put up a tent when you help each other.

5

Sport

You can play sport with friends. You need to play together as a team. These friends are playing soccer.

These friends play baseball together. They are part of a team.

Games

You can play games with your friends. These two are playing a board game.

These two are playing a card game. There are lots of different games friends can play.

Help and Share

Friends help each other. These friends are working together to make a bird house.

These friends helped each other make a cake. They had a lot of fun too.

Friends share things with each other. It's fun to share things with your friends.